The Calm Way to Publish a Book

How to Finish, Format, and Self-Publish Your Book on Amazon KDP — Without Losing Your Mind

A follow-up to The Accidental Author

Ivette Smith

Also by Ivette Smith

Nonfiction

The Accidental Author

The Dark Web and Scams

The Capability Code

The Bipolar Journey

The Bipolar Journey: Workbook Companion

Buzzing with Purpose: The Modern Beekeeper's Guide

Nature's Pharmacy: Herbal Medicine for Everyday Life

On Being a Woman

Cracks in the Foundation

The Quick Guide to Self Help

Hola, Friend!

THE CALM WAY TO PUBLISH A BOOK

How to Finish, Format, and Self-Publish Your Book on Amazon KDP — Without Losing Your Mind

Published by Ivette Smith Books

First Edition 2026

ISBN: 979-8-9950550-6-8

Table of Contents

The Calm Publishing Sequence

If you've already read The Accidental Author, you know the emotional side of writing a book. You know the strange mix of excitement and doubt that shows up during drafting. The persistence it takes to keep going when the middle gets messy. The quiet moment when the manuscript is finally finished and you realize you actually did it.

This book begins right after that moment.

Because finishing the manuscript is not the end of the journey. It's the beginning of a different phase.

Writing and publishing are not the same activity. They use different skills and require different kinds of thinking. Writing is creative work. It lives in imagination, exploration, and persistence. Publishing is operational. It involves decisions, systems, and a sequence of steps that gradually turn a manuscript into a book readers can actually find and buy.

For many first-time authors, the confusion begins because these steps appear all at once. You finish the manuscript and suddenly you're facing questions like:

- What should the title be?

- What categories should the book appear in?

- How does formatting work?

- What files does the publishing platform expect?

- What exactly are keywords and metadata?

Encountering all of those questions at the same time makes publishing feel far more complicated than it really is. But the problem usually is not complexity. It's sequence.

Most authors don't struggle with publishing because they lack capability. They struggle because no one ever shows them the order. When you don't know what comes first, everything feels urgent. When everything feels urgent, even small decisions begin to feel expensive.

This book exists to solve that problem. Instead of encountering the entire publishing system at once, we'll walk through it the way it actually works — step by step, in the order that makes the most sense.

Manuscript. Revision. Title. Cover. Formatting. Metadata. Upload. Publish.

No hype. No guru advice. Just the sequence.

Once the sequence becomes clear, the noise drops. And publishing becomes a lot calmer.

The Identity Shift

There is something else that happens when you finish a manuscript that nobody warns you about.

You stop being a writer and start being a publisher. And those two identities require different things from you.

The writer in you finished the book. The publisher in you now has to decide what to do with it. That transition can feel abrupt, especially if you spent months living inside the creative process and suddenly find yourself staring at a dashboard full of ISBNs and trim sizes.

This is normal. It is not a sign that you chose the wrong path. It is a sign that you are moving from one phase to the next.

The skills you need for publishing are learnable. They are not creative in the same way writing is, but they are finite. There is a list of things to do, and the list has an end. Unlike writing, which can always be improved, publishing has a finish line.

You will reach it.

What to Do Right Now

If you just finished a manuscript and you are reading this trying to figure out what comes next, here is the short answer.

Nothing yet.

Step away from the manuscript for at least a few days. A week is better. Two weeks is not too long.

The distance is not procrastination — it is part of
the process. You cannot see what the manuscript
actually needs while you are still inside it.

When you come back to it, you will read it
differently. You will notice things you could not see
before. That is when revision starts. And revision
is the next chapter.

Part I

The Moment After the Manuscript

The Finish Line That Isn't

Finishing a manuscript feels like a finish line.

You've been living inside this thing for months. Maybe longer. You typed the last sentence. You saved the file. You maybe even closed the laptop with slightly more force than necessary, just to make it feel official.

The book is done.

Except — and here's the part nobody tells you — it isn't.

What you actually finished is the writing. The manuscript. The first half of a two-part process.

Publishing is the second half, and it operates completely differently.

This is not a warning. It's context. The gap between finishing a manuscript and holding a published book is real, but it's not a gap of talent or intelligence. It's a gap of information. And information is fixable.

Two Different Skill Sets

Writing lives in your head. It's creative, intuitive, nonlinear. You follow an idea, you lose the thread, you find it again at 11pm, you rearrange everything, you write the same paragraph six times until it finally says what you meant. Writing rewards persistence and tolerates chaos.

Publishing does not tolerate chaos. Publishing is operational. It has a sequence, and the sequence matters.

Here's a concrete example. You finish the manuscript and decide it's time to work on the cover. You find a designer, describe the concept, and get back a file that looks good. Then you format the interior, upload it to KDP, and discover the page count is different than you expected. Which changes the spine width. Which means the cover dimensions are now wrong. Which means the cover file needs to be rebuilt.

That's not bad luck. That's doing things out of order.

Publishing asks practical questions, and most of them depend on the answers to earlier practical questions. What categories should this book appear in? What file format does KDP want? Where do ISBNs come from and do you need one? What's the difference between a trim size and a standard page size? Why is your cover upload being rejected?

These are not creative questions. They have specific answers. And when you encounter them all at the same time — which is exactly what happens when you open a publishing dashboard for the first time — it creates the feeling that publishing is a maze.

It's not a maze. It's a sequence. The problem is just that you're seeing all the steps at once instead of one at a time.

The Real Source of Publishing Overwhelm

Most authors don't struggle with publishing because they lack capability. They struggle because they lack order.

When you don't know what comes first, everything feels urgent. When everything feels urgent, even small decisions start to feel expensive. You second-guess the title. You spend three hours comparing cover designers before you've finished formatting. You try to upload a file before you understand what format it needs to be in. You read twelve articles about Amazon keywords and come away more confused than when you started.

None of that is stupidity. It's what happens when a capable person is handed a system without a map.

The publishing process is not actually that complicated. There are maybe eight major stages, and within each stage there are a handful of decisions. Most of those decisions have clear right answers, or at minimum a small number of reasonable options. The challenge is that every online resource about self-publishing seems determined to present all of it at once, out of order, with equal urgency attached to everything.

That is how you end up three hours into a YouTube rabbit hole about KDP Select versus wide distribution when you haven't even finished your table of contents.

The fix is not more information. It's better sequencing.

What Nobody Mentions About the Transition

There's one more thing worth naming before we move on.

When you finish a manuscript, something shifts. You stop being a writer — at least temporarily — and start being a publisher. These are different jobs. They require different thinking, different tools, and a different relationship with uncertainty.

Writing tolerates ambiguity. A chapter can be sort of working for a long time while you figure out what it actually needs to say. Publishing does not work that way. A file either meets the platform's specifications or it doesn't. An ISBN is either registered correctly or it isn't. The cover dimensions either match or the file gets rejected.

This shift can feel jarring, especially if you spent months in a deeply creative headspace and suddenly find yourself staring at a dashboard full of technical fields.

That feeling is normal. It doesn't mean you chose the wrong path. It means you're moving from one phase to the next, and the skills required are different.

The good news: publishing skills are learnable, finite, and teachable. Unlike writing, which you can spend a lifetime refining, publishing has a checklist. There is a specific list of things that need to happen, and when they happen in the right order, the book goes live.

That's the job. Let's walk through it.

The Sequence

Once you understand the order of operations, the whole thing gets calmer.

Here's the sequence that actually works:

- Finish the manuscript
- Revise the manuscript
- Decide on the title and subtitle
- Design the cover
- Format the interior
- Prepare metadata (description, categories, keywords)
- Upload the files
- Publish

Each step prepares the next one. When they're done in this order, the decisions are manageable. When they get scrambled, everything feels confusing.

The rest of this book walks through these stages one at a time. Starting with the step most authors try to skip: revision.

The Publishing Sequence

Before we get into the individual steps, let's look at the whole sequence.

Not because you need to memorize it — you don't — but because seeing the full picture before you start is the single most protective thing you can do for yourself. When you know where you are in the process, the noise drops. The decisions get smaller. And the whole thing starts to feel manageable instead of overwhelming.

The sequence is not a suggestion. It is the order in which things actually work.

Why Order Matters More Than You Think

Publishing is not a collection of independent tasks you can tackle whenever the mood strikes. Every step in the process depends on something that came before it. That dependency is not bureaucratic. It is structural. Skip a step or do one out of order and you do not just create extra work. You create the worst kind of extra work: the kind you have to do when you are already tired.

Think about where you will be by the time you reach the upload stage. You have been writing, revising, making cover decisions, formatting files, and navigating dashboards you have never seen before. You are not at your sharpest. You are running on the momentum of wanting this to be done.

That is exactly the wrong moment to discover that your book description — the single piece of writing that will either convert a browser into a buyer or send them scrolling past — was an afterthought you dashed off in five minutes because you just wanted to get through the setup screen.

The description is one example. There are others. The categories you pick in thirty seconds because you are impatient will determine where Amazon places your book for as long as it exists. The subtitle you write at the last minute because the title field requires one will either earn you discoverability or cost you it, every single day the book is live.

None of these are small decisions. They just feel small when you are exhausted and rushing. The sequence exists so that you make these decisions when you are calm, rested, and thinking clearly — not when you are staring at a screen at midnight trying to remember what a keyword field is.

The Cost of Rushing

Here is what actually happens when authors do things out of order.

You design the cover before locking the title. The title changes. The cover has to be rebuilt. Not tweaked — rebuilt. Because the title is not a small element on a cover. It is the largest piece of text on the front. Changing it means a new design, new file, new upload, new previewer check.

You format the interior before finishing revision. You make structural edits after formatting. Now the page breaks are wrong, the table of contents no longer matches, and the page count has changed — which means the spine width has changed — which means the cover dimensions are wrong again.

You register your ISBN before you have a final title. You enter a working title in Bowker because the field is required and you figure you can fix it later. Later turns out to be complicated. The record propagates with the wrong title. KDP sees a mismatch. You spend two days troubleshooting something that would have taken two minutes if you had waited.

You write your book description during upload because that is when KDP asks for it. You are tired. You write a summary instead of a sales pitch. You hit publish and move on. Six months later you wonder why nobody is clicking through to the book. The description is why. But now fixing it feels like going backward, and you have other things to do, so it stays broken indefinitely.

None of these scenarios are hypothetical. They are what happens. Not to careless authors. To capable, intelligent authors who simply did not know the order mattered this much.

The Full Map

Here is the sequence. Read it once before you start. Come back to it whenever you feel the urge to skip ahead.

- Manuscript — The writing is done. You have a complete draft.

- Revision — You tighten it, fix what's broken, make it readable for someone who isn't you.

- Title and Subtitle — You decide how the book positions itself in the market. You lock these before anything else moves forward.

- Cover — You create the visual signal that tells readers what kind of book they're looking at. Cover design starts after the title is locked. Not before.

- Formatting — You prepare the interior for both print and ebook. Formatting happens after revision is complete. Not during.

- Metadata — Description, categories, and keywords. This is how Amazon finds your readers. Written deliberately, in advance, not typed into a field while you're trying to finish the upload.

- ISBN Registration — Purchased and fully registered in Bowker, with all fields completed, before you open KDP.

- Upload — You push the files to KDP and review everything carefully in the previewer before it goes live.

- Publish — You click the button. The book exists in the world.

Each step prepares the next one. When they are done in this order, each decision is the right size for the moment you are making it. When they get scrambled, small decisions become expensive ones because you are making them under pressure with incomplete information.

The Decisions That Deserve Your Best Thinking

Some steps in the publishing process are technical. They have right answers and wrong answers, and once you know what they are, they are not that hard. Page size is either correct or it isn't. The gutter margin either meets KDP's minimum or it doesn't. These things are fixable and the fixes are straightforward.

Other steps are strategic. They require judgment, clarity, and real thought. The title. The subtitle. The book description. The categories. These are the decisions that will determine whether your book finds its readers or disappears into the catalog noise.

Here is the thing about strategic decisions: they look exactly the same as technical ones when you are in the middle of an upload. They are just fields in a dashboard. They all feel equally urgent. And if you have not thought about them in advance, you will make them the same way you make technical decisions — quickly, under pressure, trying to get through the screen.

That is how authors end up with book descriptions that read like plot summaries. That is how subtitle fields get filled with whatever sounds reasonable at 11pm. That is how categories get picked based on what seems close enough rather than what actually fits.

The sequence protects you from that. When you work through title and subtitle before you ever open the dashboard, you are making that decision at your best — with time to research, test, and get it right. When you draft your book description as a standalone piece of writing rather than a form field, it reads like writing. When you research categories before you need them, you pick the right ones instead of the first ones that look acceptable.

Give your best thinking to the decisions that deserve it. The sequence makes sure you are not being asked for your best thinking at the worst possible moment.

A Note on Revision

Some authors try to skip revision entirely. That is their call to make.

What I will say is this: the authors who skip it almost always wish they hadn't. Not because the first draft is terrible — sometimes it is excellent — but because distance from the manuscript reveals things you cannot see when you are still inside it. Sentences that made perfect sense in the flow of writing read as confusing to a fresh eye. Sections that felt essential turn out to be redundant. Things you meant to say clearly turn out to need one more pass.

Even a few days away changes what you notice. A week is better. You do not need to be perfect. You just need to be clear. Give yourself enough time to read it like a reader, not like the person who wrote it. Then move on.

A Word About Timelines

New authors often ask how long the publishing process takes.

The honest answer is that it depends almost entirely on how long revision takes and how quickly you make decisions. The technical steps — formatting, cover creation, upload — can be done in a few focused days once the manuscript is final and the strategic decisions are already made. Revision takes as long as it takes. Some books need a week. Some need two months.

Do not rush revision to speed up publishing. A well-revised manuscript that takes six weeks to prepare is a better book than a poorly revised one that publishes in two. The book will be available for as long as you want it to be. Getting it right is worth the time.

The same goes for every other step in the sequence. Rushing the description to get through the upload screen saves you twenty minutes today and costs you readers for the lifetime of the book. Waiting until you are rested and clear-headed to write it takes twenty minutes and serves you for years.

Calm publishing is not slow publishing. It is publishing done in the right order, at the right moment, with the right amount of attention on the things that actually matter.

That is the whole point of the sequence. Let's walk through it.

Part II

The Decisions That Shape the Book

Titles, Subtitles, and Discoverability

Here's something most authors don't fully register until after they've published:

Your title is metadata.

It's also the name of your book and the first impression it makes on a stranger. But before any of that, it's one of the primary signals Amazon uses to decide when and where to show your book in search results.

That doesn't mean your title has to be boring. It means it has to be clear. And those two things are not the same.

The Job of a Title

A title has one job: tell a cold stranger what the book is about.

Not what it means to you. Not what inspired it. Not the metaphor you built the whole manuscript around. What it is. What it covers. What it helps with.

This sounds obvious until you start looking at how many nonfiction authors bury the actual subject behind something clever, poetic, or meaningful-only-to-them. The problem is not that those titles are bad writing. The problem is that they were written for someone who already knows what the book is about. They were written for you. Not for the reader who is scrolling Amazon at 10pm looking for exactly what you wrote.

A title that requires decoding is a title that loses readers in the three seconds they spend deciding whether to click. By the time the meaning lands, they have already moved on.

Clarity beats cleverness. Every time. Sorry.

The Trap of the Meaningful Title

Here is the thing nobody says out loud: the title you fall in love with during drafting is usually the wrong one.

You've been living inside this manuscript for months. Every word of the title carries weight for you. It means something. It captures the essence of what you wrote in a way that feels true and resonant and exactly right.

And to a stranger on Amazon, it means nothing.

I've made this mistake myself. Several times, actually. Looking back at my own catalog, I can point to titles that made complete sense to me when I wrote them and do almost no discoverability work at all.

On Being a Woman. That title feels meaningful. It feels honest. It feels like something. But type those words into Amazon and you will get back a hundred books about a hundred different things. The title tells a reader nothing specific about what the book covers, who it's for, or what problem it solves. The reader who needs that book cannot find it because nothing in the title speaks to what she's actually searching for.

Cracks in the Foundation has the same problem, just with more poetry. Could be a home repair guide. Could be a memoir. Could be a thriller. The title is doing zero discoverability work. Someone who already knows I wrote it understands what it means. Nobody else does.

The Quick Guide to Self Help has the opposite problem. Too generic. Every word in that title is a high-competition search term owned by authors with bigger catalogs and more reviews. The title isn't wrong — it's just invisible for a completely different reason. Instead of being too specific to find, it's too broad to rank.

And then there's Hola, Friend! — a charming title that signals exactly the right tone and absolutely none of the searchable content. The reader looking for a Spanish learning book does not type "hola friend" into Amazon. They type "learn Spanish for beginners" or "conversational Spanish guide." The title is friendly and warm and completely invisible to the algorithm.

Four different books. Four different failure modes. Too vague. Too poetic. Too generic. Too cute. All of them felt right when I wrote them. None of them are doing the work they should be doing.

This is not a confession of incompetence. It is an extremely common experience. The authors who avoid it are the ones who step outside themselves early enough to ask: what would a stranger search for, and does my title answer that search?

Subtitles Do the Heavy Lifting

In nonfiction, the subtitle is where you earn your discoverability.

Think of it this way: the title is the hook, the subtitle is the explanation. The title makes someone look. The subtitle makes them click.

A good subtitle does three things simultaneously. It clarifies exactly what the book covers. It communicates the benefit to the reader. And it includes words that readers actually type into search bars.

Take this book as an example. The Calm Way to Publish a Book sounds appealing, but it doesn't tell you much on its own. The subtitle — How to Finish, Format, and Self-Publish Your Book on Amazon KDP Without Losing Your Mind — tells you what you'll learn, what problem it solves, and includes terms like self-publish, format, and Amazon KDP that people actually type when they are looking for exactly this kind of help.

Your subtitle is doing work your title probably cannot do alone. And if you wrote your subtitle in five minutes right before you hit publish, you almost certainly left discoverability on the table.

How to Actually Write a Subtitle

Most authors treat the subtitle as an afterthought. They finish the manuscript, pick a title they like, and then dash off a subtitle that roughly describes the content. That is not how a subtitle should be built.

Start with the reader's problem. What is the specific frustration, confusion, or need that brought them to Amazon in the first place? That is the language your subtitle should speak.

Then think about the outcome. What does the reader have, know, or feel after reading the book that they didn't before? That is your benefit statement.

Then check the words. Are the specific terms in your subtitle the ones readers actually search for? Not your industry language. Not your preferred phrasing. The words a slightly frustrated person types into a search bar when they need help with the thing your book covers.

A subtitle that hits all three — problem, outcome, searchable language — is doing its job. A subtitle that misses any one of them is leaving readers behind.

How Amazon Actually Reads Your Title

Amazon's search algorithm weighs metadata in a rough priority order. Title and subtitle are at the top of that list — they carry more weight than your keyword fields, your categories, or your book description.

This means if you have a search term you really want to rank for, the best place for it is not in your keyword fields. It is in your subtitle. The algorithm trusts title and subtitle more than it trusts the keyword slots because authors tend to game keyword fields. The title and subtitle are harder to stuff without making the book look ridiculous.

We'll go deeper on the algorithm in Chapter 4, but for now: your subtitle is one of the most valuable pieces of real estate on your entire book page. Treat it that way.

> *Algorithm priority order: Title → Subtitle → Keywords → Categories → Description. Your most important search terms belong as high up that list as possible.*

The Little Things You Think About and Forget

There is a category of title mistakes that are not about strategy. They are about the small things that seem fine in the moment and surface as problems later. Here is the list nobody gives you.

You tested the title on people who already know what the book is about. Of course they said it was clear. They already knew. The test that matters is showing the title and subtitle to someone who knows nothing about the manuscript and asking them to tell you what the book covers and who it's for. If they get it right, you're good. If they hesitate or guess wrong, something needs to change.

You didn't check whether another book already owns that title in your category. Search your exact title on Amazon before you finalize it. If a well-reviewed book with the same title is already ranking in your category, you are going to spend your entire launch fighting to be seen next to it. Pick a title with less competition.

The title works great said out loud but looks strange in text. Some titles have a rhythm or a play on words that only works when spoken. In text, especially at thumbnail size on a phone screen, they flatten out and read as confusing. Read your title silently, as a stranger would read it. Does it still work?

The subtitle is too long to display cleanly. Amazon truncates long subtitles in certain display contexts. If your subtitle is a full sentence with multiple clauses, parts of it may get cut off before the reader sees the most important words. Front-load the searchable terms. Put the clever part at the end, not the beginning.

You used your own terminology instead of the reader's. Every field has its own vocabulary, and the vocabulary experts use is often different from the vocabulary beginners search for. If your book is for people who don't yet know the specialized terms, your title and subtitle need to speak the language they have right now — not the language they'll have after reading your book.

You picked the title when you were still inside the manuscript. The title that feels right at the end of a long drafting session is often the title that captures what the book means to you. Step away. Come back in a week and read your title as if someone else wrote it. Ask whether it still makes sense to a stranger. Often it does not.

How to Test Your Title

Before you lock a title, run it through a simple sequence.

First, search for it on Amazon. Not to see if it exists — though that is useful to know — but to see what comes up. Do the results look like your book's neighbors? Do they signal the same genre, the same audience, the same kind of content? If the search results look right, that is a good sign. If they pull up books in completely different categories, something in your title is sending the wrong signal.

Second, check Amazon autocomplete. Type the first few words of your subtitle into the Amazon search bar and watch what it suggests. Those suggestions are drawn from what real readers are actually typing. If your subtitle language appears in the autocomplete, you are using the right words. If it doesn't, consider whether there is a more natural phrasing that matches what readers search for.

Third, do the cold stranger test. Show the title and subtitle to someone who has not read the manuscript and has no context for what the book is about. Ask them: what do you think this book covers, and who is it for? If they get it right, the title is working. If they are not sure, something needs to be clearer. It is almost always the subtitle.

How Your Title Looks in a List

Here is something that almost never comes up in publishing advice: your title has to work in a list.

When a reader lands on your Amazon author page, they see all of your books at once. A reader who found one title and liked it is now scanning the rest of your catalog deciding what to read next. At that moment, your titles are competing not with other authors' books but with each other.

If every title in your catalog is vague and poetic, the catalog reads as a blur. Nothing stands out. Nothing signals clearly what each book is about. The reader who might have bought three books buys one and leaves.

If your titles are specific and clear, the reader can scan the list and immediately identify which books apply to their situation. They might not buy them all today. But they know which ones to come back for.

This is one of the reasons building a catalog with consistent naming conventions pays off over time. Readers learn the pattern. They know what to expect from you. And when a new title appears that fits the pattern, the click feels natural.

Series Titles and Consistency

If this book is part of a series or a follow-up to another title, your naming convention matters more than it might seem.

Amazon's algorithm connects books by the same author, and readers who find one book in a series will often look for others. Making the relationship between the titles clear — either through explicit numbering, consistent subtitle structure, or shared language — helps that discovery happen organically.

This book is a follow-up to The Accidental Author. Both titles use plain, direct language. Both subtitles follow the same structure: here is what you will learn, here is what problem it solves. A reader who finished The Accidental Author and found it useful can look at this title and understand immediately that it is the next step. The connection is visible without having to be explained.

You do not need to be heavy-handed about it. But if a reader finishes one of your books and wants more from you, the path to the next book should be obvious from the title alone.

Locking the Title Before You Move On

Don't finalize your title too early in the process, and don't leave it undecided too long.

A working title is fine during drafting. But before you move into cover design, you need a locked title — because the cover designer, or you if you're doing it yourself, needs to know exactly what words are going on the front. Changes to the title after the cover is designed mean redesigning the cover. That costs time and sometimes money.

The title also shapes your description, your keyword strategy, and your category selection. Every downstream decision in the publishing process is influenced by what the title says. The sooner it is locked, the fewer things you have to redo later.

Get it settled before the next step. Then move forward and don't second-guess it.

Categories, Keywords, and the Algorithm

Let's talk about the part of publishing that makes most authors' eyes glaze over.

Metadata.

I know. But stay with me, because this is actually the part where a lot of books quietly succeed or fail without the author ever understanding why.

How Amazon Decides Where Your Book Shows Up

Amazon isn't psychic. It doesn't read your book. It reads your metadata — the information you enter into the publishing dashboard — and uses that to decide when and where to surface your book in search results.

The fields it weighs, in rough order of importance:

- Title — Highest weight. Words here matter most.

- Subtitle — Nearly as important as the title. Use it.

- Keywords — Seven slots. Choose them deliberately.

- Categories — Two slots. They determine your browse placement.

- Description — Matters for conversion, not primarily for search ranking.

The Keyword Fields

You get seven keyword fields. Each one can hold a phrase, not just a single word.

A few rules that will save you from wasting them:

- Don't repeat words already in your title or subtitle. Amazon already has those — you're not adding anything by duplicating them.

- Think in phrases, not single words. "Self-publishing guide for beginners" is more useful than "publishing."

- Think like a reader typing into a search bar at 10pm, slightly frustrated, looking for a specific answer. What do they type?

- Avoid keywords that are too broad (book) or too competitive (Amazon) unless you have a very specific reason.

You can change your keywords after publishing. If something isn't working, you can adjust. This is not a permanent decision carved in stone — it's a dial you can turn.

The Category Slots

You choose two categories during setup. These determine where your book appears in Amazon's browse structure — the virtual shelves.

Two thoughts on this:

First, be specific. A book in "Self-Help > Writing Skills" is going to have a harder time standing out than the same book in a more targeted subcategory. Drill down as far as the category tree lets you go.

Second, you can request additional categories after publishing by contacting KDP support. Most authors don't know this. Most authors also don't do it. You should do it.

The Description

Your description is not a summary of your book.

It's a sales pitch.

There's a meaningful difference. A summary tells readers what the book contains. A sales pitch tells readers why they need it.

Lead with the problem your reader is experiencing. Then tell them what the book does about it. Keep it tight — most readers don't scroll to the bottom of long descriptions.

We'll go deeper on description writing in Chapter 10 when we walk through the KDP metadata fields. For now, just know that "description" means "the thing that convinces someone who is already looking at your book to actually buy it."

How to Research Keywords

The best keywords are the ones your actual readers are already using.

Start by searching Amazon for books similar to yours. Look at their titles, subtitles, and descriptions. What language do they use? What phrases show up repeatedly? Those phrases are signals that readers in your category are using that language to find books.

You can also use the Amazon search bar itself as a research tool. Type a few words related to your book and watch what autocomplete suggests. Those suggestions are based on what people are actually searching for. They are the words your readers type when they are looking for exactly what you wrote.

Use that language. Not your language. Theirs.

Updating Metadata After Publication

Here is something most publishing guides do not tell you: your metadata is not permanent.

You can change your keywords at any time from your KDP bookshelf. You can request category changes by contacting KDP support. You can rewrite your description without taking the book down.

This means your first set of metadata choices does not have to be perfect. It has to be good enough to get the book into the right neighborhood. Then you watch what happens, see what is working, and adjust.

Authors who treat metadata as a one-time decision often leave significant discoverability on the table. The ones who revisit it every few months, update keywords based on what is actually driving traffic, and refine their descriptions based on what converts — those are the authors whose back catalogs keep selling.

Covers That Signal the Right Reader

Let me reframe cover design for you before we go any further.

A book cover is not art.

It's packaging.

The goal isn't to express yourself or impress other designers. The goal is to get the right reader to recognize, in about two seconds, that this book might be for them. That's the entire job.

What a Cover Actually Communicates

Before a reader reads your title, before they read your subtitle, before they look at your description — they see the cover. And in that fraction of a second, the cover is answering a question the reader didn't consciously ask:

What kind of book is this?

Genre. Tone. Audience. All of that gets communicated visually, instantly, before a single word is processed.

This is why covers within a genre tend to look similar. That's not lazy design — it's intentional signaling. Readers learn to recognize the visual language of genres they love. When a cover speaks that language, the right reader feels it.

When a cover doesn't speak that language — when it looks like something from a different genre, or like nothing in particular — readers scroll past.

The Thumbnail Test

Here's the test that actually matters.

Find your cover and shrink it to approximately the size it appears in an Amazon search result. About an inch tall, maybe less. That tiny rectangle is the first impression most readers will have of your book.

At that size, ask yourself:

- Can you read the title?

- Does the overall image still communicate something?

- Does it look like it belongs in its genre?

If the title disappears at thumbnail size, you have a problem. Complex artwork often falls apart at small sizes. Clear typography and simple design tend to survive the shrink.

The Bookstore Test

Imagine your book on a shelf. A reader walks past and glances at it for two seconds.

Without picking it up, can they answer:

- What kind of book is this?

- Who is it for?

- What does it help with?

If the answer to any of those is "I'm not sure," the cover needs work.

DIY or Hire It Out

Both can work. I'm not going to tell you that you absolutely must hire a professional, because I've seen professionally designed covers that were confusing and DIY covers that were exactly right.

What I will say: if you go DIY, simplicity is your best friend and depending on your budget, you can use OpenAI or the image generator in ChatGPT. Clear title. Readable font. Design that doesn't fight itself. Look at covers in your genre and understand what they're doing before you start designing.

If you hire someone, show them examples of covers you like. Don't just describe what you want — show them. Designers work better from visual references than from written descriptions.

Either way: clarity over cleverness. The right reader needs to recognize your book, not decode it.

The Back Cover

Most authors spend all their energy on the front cover and treat the back as an afterthought.

That is a mistake.

The back cover is where the reader who is already interested makes their final decision. They picked it up. They looked at the front. Now they are flipping it over. What they read in the next ten seconds determines whether they buy it.

A strong back cover has three elements: a hook that immediately resonates with the reader's problem, a brief description that tells them what the book delivers, and a closing line that makes them want to start reading right now.

Keep it tight. Back covers are not the place for long paragraphs. Use white space. Make it easy to skim. The reader's eye needs to land on the most important thing first.

Working With a Cover Designer

If you are hiring a designer, a few things will save you both time.

Know your genre before you have the conversation. Send the designer five to ten covers in your category that you think work well. Do not describe the aesthetic — show it. Designers read visual references faster than verbal descriptions, and giving them examples prevents the most common source of miscommunication.

Agree on the number of revision rounds upfront. Most designers include two or three rounds in their base fee. Know what happens if you need more.

Deliver your final title and subtitle before the designer starts. Changes to text after the design is done cost time and sometimes money.

Get the final files in the formats you need: a print-ready PDF at 300 DPI for the full wraparound cover, and a separate front-cover image for the ebook. Not all designers deliver both automatically. Ask before you sign off.

Part III

The Formatting Maze

The Tools

Before we go any further, it's worth admitting something.

Most authors spend at least a little time worrying that they are using the wrong tool.

They read forums. They watch videos. They compare software options and wonder whether buying a new program will somehow make the publishing process easier. The internet has strong opinions about this and almost none of them agree. Vellum versus Atticus. Word versus LibreOffice. Scrivener versus everything. Everyone has a preference and everyone is convinced theirs is correct.

Meanwhile the manuscript is sitting there waiting.

Here is what becomes clear after you have been through the process a few times: the tool is almost never the problem. The manuscript is the problem. And no tool, no matter how well designed, can fix a manuscript that was not ready to be formatted in the first place.

The Accidental Good Result

Here is something that happens to a lot of authors and almost nobody talks about.

You format your first book. Something about the way you wrote it — the heading styles you happened to use, the way you structured the chapters, some combination of factors you did not consciously choose — lines up with what the tool expects. The output looks good. The book uploads cleanly. You think you understand how the tool works.

Then you format the second book. Same tool. Same process, as far as you can tell. The output is a mess. Spacing is wrong. Chapter breaks are in the wrong places. Headings are behaving differently than they did last time. You spend hours trying to figure out what changed.

What changed was the manuscript. The first one happened to be clean in the ways the tool needed. The second one wasn't. But because you never knew why the first one worked, you have no way to diagnose why the second one didn't.

This is the accidental good result trap. You got the right outcome without understanding the reason, so you have no repeatable process. Every book becomes a fresh gamble.

The way out of the trap is understanding what the tool actually needs from you before you hand it your manuscript.

What Atticus Actually Needs

Atticus is a good tool. It is designed specifically for authors, it handles a lot of the layout work automatically, and it can produce clean, professional book files without requiring you to understand typography or page design.

But Atticus has a requirement that is not obvious from the marketing materials: it needs your manuscript to be structured before it can format it. Not roughly structured. Not mostly structured. Consistently and correctly structured, from the first page to the last.

What that means in practice is this. Every chapter title needs to be tagged as Heading 1. Every section header needs to be tagged as Heading 2. Every paragraph of body text needs to be in Normal style. No exceptions, no mixing, no "I'll fix the inconsistent ones later."

If your manuscript has chapter titles formatted by making the text larger and bold instead of applying a heading style, Atticus does not see them as chapter titles. It sees them as large bold body text. The chapter breaks do not happen where you expect. The table of contents does not generate correctly. The navigation does not work.

If your body text has extra blank lines between paragraphs instead of paragraph spacing built into the style, Atticus formats those blank lines as content. You get double spacing in places you did not intend and inconsistent spacing throughout.

If some chapters use tab indents for the first line of each paragraph and others use paragraph indents set in the style, Atticus treats them differently. The result looks inconsistent even though you did not intend it to be.

None of this is Atticus failing. It is Atticus doing exactly what it was designed to do — formatting whatever structure it finds in your manuscript. If the structure is inconsistent, the output will be inconsistent. The tool cannot fix what the manuscript did not set up correctly.

The "I'll Fix It Later" Tax

There is a very human tendency when you are deep in the flow of writing to notice a formatting inconsistency, think "I'll fix that later," and keep writing.

Later always comes. And when it comes, it is never at a good time.

Later is when you are tired from finishing the manuscript. Later is when you are impatient to get the book uploaded. Later is when you have already been staring at the file for three days and you just want it to be done. Later is the worst possible time to go back through a 200-page document fixing every heading style and removing every manual spacing override and replacing every tab indent with a proper paragraph indent.

The tax for "I'll fix it later" is paid at the most expensive moment, in the most expensive currency: your attention and your patience, when you have the least of both.

Every inconsistency you let slide during drafting is a problem you are deferring to your most exhausted future self. That future self will not thank you. She is going to be sitting there at midnight wondering why Atticus is producing something broken and whether she has to reformat the entire manuscript from scratch.

The answer, usually, is yes.

The Template Problem

The solution to all of this is a template. A single document, set up once, with all the styles already configured correctly — Heading 1 for chapter titles, Heading 2 for section headers, Normal for body text, all the spacing built into the styles rather than inserted manually. You open the template, you write, and the structure is already there. When you hand the file to Atticus, it sees exactly what it needs.

Most authors know this. Most authors do not do it.

The reason is not laziness, exactly. It is that templates feel like work before the writing starts, and when you are ready to write, the last thing you want to do is configure a document. So you open a blank file, start typing, and tell yourself you will sort out the formatting before you format.

You will not sort out the formatting before you format. You will write the whole book in whatever state the blank file started in, accumulate every inconsistency that comes naturally from a long drafting process, and then face the entire cleanup job at once.

A template removes that problem entirely. Not by making formatting exciting. By making it invisible.

You do the setup once, correctly, and then you never think about it again. Every book you write after that starts from a clean, properly structured document that any formatting tool can work with.

What a Ready-to-Format Manuscript Looks Like

Whether you use a template from the start or clean up a finished manuscript before formatting, here is what the file needs to look like before you hand it to any tool.

Every chapter title is tagged as Heading 1. Not made larger. Not made bold. Tagged with the Heading 1 style in your word processor. This is what tells the formatting tool where chapters begin and what to use for the table of contents.

Every section header within a chapter is tagged as Heading 2. Consistent throughout the entire manuscript. If some section headers are Heading 2 and others are just bold Normal text, the tool will treat them differently.

Every paragraph of body text is in Normal style. Not Default. Not Body Text. Normal. And Normal should have paragraph spacing built into it — space after each paragraph — so you are not using blank lines to create visual separation.

No tab indents. First-line indents, if you use them, should be set in the paragraph style, not created by pressing Tab at the start of each paragraph. Tab indents are invisible inconsistencies that cause visible formatting problems.

No manual page breaks in the middle of chapters. Page breaks between chapters are fine. A manual page break inserted because text was landing awkwardly during drafting will land just as awkwardly — or more so — when the tool reformats the document for a different page size.

No double spaces after periods. If you learned to type with two spaces after a period, find and replace them all before formatting. Two spaces after a period produces inconsistent spacing in justified text.

That is the list. It is not complicated. It is tedious to retrofit onto a manuscript that was not written this way. It takes about twenty minutes to set up correctly at the start of a new document and zero minutes to maintain once it is there.

The Tools Authors Actually Use

With that context, here is a brief honest look at the tools most authors encounter.

Microsoft Word is what many authors already have. It is perfectly capable of producing a properly formatted manuscript if styles and spacing are handled correctly. Its main liability is that it makes it very easy to format things manually — to bold a heading instead of applying a style, to press Enter twice instead of setting paragraph spacing — and those manual choices accumulate into exactly the kind of inconsistency that breaks formatting tools downstream.

LibreOffice is a free alternative that performs most of the same functions. Everything said about Word applies here. The tool is capable. The manuscript still has to be clean.

Atticus is purpose-built for authors and handles a lot of the layout decisions automatically. It is the right tool for many independent authors. It requires a clean, consistently styled manuscript to work correctly. Feed it a well-structured file and it will produce a professional result. Feed it a messy one and it will format the mess professionally.

Vellum produces beautiful book interiors with minimal effort and is widely used by independent authors. It is Mac-only, which eliminates it for a portion of authors immediately. Like Atticus, it works best with a clean manuscript.

Scrivener is excellent for drafting and organizing complex manuscripts. It is not a formatting tool. Most authors who draft in Scrivener compile their manuscript to a Word or DOCX file before formatting. The compile step can introduce its own inconsistencies, so review the compiled file before handing it to a formatting tool.

The Free Path

Nobody talks about this enough: you do not have to buy specialized software to publish a professional-looking book.

LibreOffice is free. KDP provides free formatting templates for the most common trim sizes, downloadable directly from the KDP website. A clean manuscript in a KDP template, exported as PDF, produces a file that uploads correctly and looks professional.

And then there is Kindle Create, which Amazon provides for free and which almost nobody mentions.

Kindle Create is Amazon's own formatting app. It is simple, it is free, and it is not bad. That last part surprises people. There is a tendency to assume that free tools from the platform are bare-minimum consolation prizes. Kindle Create is genuinely easy to use. You import your manuscript, apply the formatting, preview the result, and export the file. It handles both ebook and print formatting and it is designed specifically to produce files that KDP accepts without issues — because Amazon built it for exactly that purpose.

If you are new to formatting and you do not want to spend money on tools before you know whether you need them, start with Kindle Create. Download it, import your manuscript, and see what it does. You may find that it handles everything you need. You may outgrow it as your books get more complex. But as a starting point, especially for authors publishing their first or second book, it is a legitimate option that costs nothing and works.

The free path requires more manual attention to formatting details than a dedicated tool like Atticus or Vellum. But it works. Plenty of authors publish clean, professional books this way. If budget is a constraint or you want to understand the formatting process before investing in tools, start here.

What to Check When the Tool Gives You a File

Whatever tool you use, there are things you need to verify before you upload the output file to KDP. Most authors export the file, glance at it, and upload. That is how formatting problems end up in published books.

Open the output file and check these things. Chapter titles are all present and formatted consistently. No chapters are missing or merged together. Section headers look the same throughout. Body text spacing is consistent — no random gaps or compressed sections. Page numbers are present. The table of contents has entries for every chapter. No pages are blank that should not be blank. The first page of each chapter starts on the correct side.

Then upload it to KDP and check it again in the previewer. The previewer is the final test. What looks correct in your word processor does not always survive the conversion process intact. The previewer shows you what KDP actually has. Trust the previewer over everything else.

The tool is the last step in a process that starts with a clean manuscript. Get the manuscript right first. Everything after that gets easier.

Interior Layout Without Headaches

By the time authors reach this stage, a quiet fear usually appears.

Formatting.

Somewhere along the way, formatting acquired a reputation as one of the most mysterious parts of publishing. Forums are full of horror stories about broken layouts, rejected uploads, and files that look fine on one screen but fall apart on another.

Some of that reputation is earned. There is one formatting trap in particular that catches almost every first-time author and causes a chain reaction that reaches all the way to the cover. Understanding it before you start will save you more time and frustration than almost anything else in this book.

The Page Size Trap

When you open a new document in Word or LibreOffice, it defaults to 8.5 by 11 inches. That is the standard US letter size. It is what the software assumes you want because most people using a word processor are writing documents, not books.

Nothing on screen tells you this is wrong for a book. There is no warning. There is no prompt asking what trim size you intend to publish at. The page looks like a page. You write your book. It looks fine the entire time you are writing it.

Then you upload it to KDP and select a trim size of 6 by 9 inches — the most common size for nonfiction. And KDP takes your 8.5 by 11 document and tries to fit it into a 6 by 9 book.

The page count changes. Sometimes dramatically. A manuscript that was 180 pages at 8.5 by 11 might become 260 pages at 6 by 9, depending on fonts, margins, and spacing. Or it might compress. Either way, the page count you see in your word processor is not the page count KDP will produce, and that number matters more than most authors realize.

Here is why: your spine width is calculated from your page count. The spine width determines the total dimensions of your cover file. If the page count changes after you have already built the cover, the cover dimensions are wrong. The spine is too narrow or too wide. KDP will reject it or the printed book will have a cover that does not wrap correctly.

So the chain looks like this. Wrong page size in your document leads to wrong page count in KDP. Wrong page count means wrong spine width. Wrong spine width means the cover has to be rebuilt. And rebuilding a cover is not a small fix — it means recalculating the dimensions, adjusting the design, re-exporting the file, re-uploading, and going through the previewer again.

All of that because the document started at the wrong page size.

The XML Nobody Told You About

Here is what makes this trap particularly frustrating: the page size is not just a setting you can see and change easily. It is embedded in the document itself, in the underlying file structure, and your word processor does not surface it prominently.

In Word and LibreOffice, the page dimensions are stored in the document's XML — the underlying code that defines how the file is structured. When you format a document and export it as PDF or DOCX, those embedded dimensions travel with the file. KDP reads them. If they say 8.5 by 11, that is what KDP works with regardless of what trim size you selected in the dashboard.

The fix is straightforward but it has to happen before you format, not after. In Word, go to Layout, then Size, and set the page dimensions to your trim size — 6 by 9 for most nonfiction. In LibreOffice, go to Format, then Page Style, and change the width and height there. Do this before you do anything else. Before you set margins. Before you format headings. Before you worry about fonts.

The cleanest approach is to start from a KDP template. Amazon provides free formatting templates for every trim size they support, downloadable from the KDP help pages. These templates already have the correct page dimensions baked in. They also have pre-set margins that meet KDP's minimums. Starting from a template means the page size problem never occurs because the correct dimensions are already there.

If you are cleaning up an existing manuscript that was written at the wrong size, the safest approach is to open a new document at the correct trim size, copy your text in, and reapply your styles. It feels like extra work. It is less work than reformatting after a failed upload.

Why Page Count Matters So Much

The page count of your finished, formatted interior is not just a number. It drives several downstream decisions that authors often do not anticipate.

Spine width is the most immediate. KDP provides a spine width calculator and the formula is simple: multiply your page count by the paper thickness factor for your chosen paper type, then add the cover thickness. KDP's cover template generator does this math for you once you enter your page count and paper type. But you cannot enter your page count until you have a formatted interior at the correct trim size. Which means the cover cannot be finalized until the interior is done.

This is the correct order. Interior first. Page count from the interior. Cover dimensions from the page count. Cover design and export last. Authors who try to build the cover before finishing the interior almost always have to rebuild it.

Gutter margin is the second thing page count affects. The gutter is the inside margin — the edge of the page closest to the spine. Print books need a larger inside margin than outside margin because some of that space disappears into the binding. The thicker the book, the more space the binding consumes, and the larger the gutter needs to be. KDP enforces minimum gutter requirements based on page count. A book under 150 pages needs a gutter of at least 0.375 inches. A book between 300 and 500 pages needs at least 0.75 inches. If you set your gutter before you know your page count, you may be setting it wrong.

Pricing is the third factor. KDP's printing cost is calculated partly by page count. More pages cost more to print. If your royalty calculation assumed a certain page count and the actual count comes in significantly different, your pricing may need to adjust.

None of these are unsolvable problems. They are all fixable. But they are much easier to handle correctly the first time than to correct after the fact.

Mirror Margins and Why Print Books Need Them

When you set up margins for a print book, you are not setting one margin for all pages. You are setting different margins for left-hand pages and right-hand pages.

This is called mirror margins, and it is how every professionally printed book is set up. The outside margin — the edge away from the spine — is the same on both sides. The inside margin — the edge toward the spine — is also the same on both sides, but larger than the outside margin because it needs to account for the binding.

In Word, turn on mirror margins in the Page Setup dialog under the Margins tab. In LibreOffice, go to Format, Page Style, and set the inner and outer margins separately. Once mirror margins are enabled, your document will show alternating left and right page layouts, which is correct.

If you set up your margins without mirror margins enabled, your gutter will be on the wrong side for half the pages in your book. The inside edge of every left-hand page will have the smaller margin, and the binding will eat into your text.

The Numbers That Matter

For a 6 by 9 inch book, here are the margin settings that work and meet KDP's minimums.

Outside margin: 0.75 inches. Top margin: 0.75 inches. Bottom margin: 0.75 inches. Inside margin (gutter): 0.375 inches for books under 150 pages, 0.5 inches for books between 151 and 300 pages, 0.75 inches for books between 301 and 500 pages, and 0.875 inches for books over 500 pages.

For fonts, a serif font at 11 or 12 points reads comfortably in print. Georgia, Garamond, and Palatino are all solid choices. Avoid decorative or display fonts for body text. Avoid sans-serif fonts for long-form body text in print — they fatigue readers on the printed page even if they look clean on screen.

Line spacing between 1.15 and 1.5 gives the page breathing room without feeling airy. Use paragraph spacing of 6 to 10 points after each paragraph instead of pressing Enter twice between paragraphs. Built-in paragraph spacing is cleaner and does not create the blank-line formatting problems described in the previous chapter.

Five Formatting Mistakes Almost Every First-Time Author Makes

Beyond the page size trap, here are the other problems that show up most consistently.

Formatting before revision is complete. Every structural edit you make after formatting — adding a section, moving a chapter, cutting several pages — shifts the layout and may change the page count. Format when the manuscript is stable. Not before.

Using manual spacing instead of style-based spacing. Pressing Enter twice to create space between paragraphs, or pressing Tab to indent the first line, creates invisible inconsistencies that format unpredictably. Build spacing into your paragraph styles and use them consistently.

Inconsistent heading styles. A chapter title formatted as Heading 1 in Chapter 1 and as large bold Normal text in Chapter 3 will behave differently in every tool that touches the file. Apply heading styles consistently from the first page to the last.

Ignoring the table of contents. In ebooks especially, the table of contents is how readers navigate. A properly linked table of contents requires correct heading styles throughout the manuscript. If the headings are inconsistent, the table of contents will be incomplete or wrong.

Elaborate formatting that does not survive ebook conversion. Drop shadows, custom fonts, complex layouts, and decorative elements that look intentional in print often become garbled in ebook format. Keep the ebook version simple. The reader's device controls most of the visual presentation anyway.

Print Versus Ebook Formatting

Print formatting is fixed. Every element stays exactly where you put it. The reader has no control over how the page looks. This is why print layout requires careful attention to margins, fonts, spacing, and page count — whatever you set is what every reader sees.

Ebook formatting is fluid. The reader can change the font size, the typeface, the line spacing, and the background color. Whatever you lock down in your ebook file will be partially or fully overridden by the reader's preferences and device settings.

This is why elaborate print layouts do not translate to ebooks. The reader's device will ignore most of them. For ebooks, keep it simple. Clear headings, clean paragraph breaks, and proper chapter navigation are what matter. Do not try to replicate your print layout in the ebook file. Let the text flow naturally.

Format the print interior first. Get the page count. Build the cover. Then format the ebook as a separate, simpler version of the same content.

Formatting Is the Last Structural Step

Once the interior layout is complete, something happens that does not happen at any earlier stage.

The manuscript looks like a book.

The chapters sit on pages at the right size. The table of contents works. The margins give the text room to breathe. The structure becomes visible in a way that a draft document never quite achieves.

At that point you have three things that exist together for the first time: a finished manuscript, a formatted interior, and a page count you can trust. The cover can now be built to the correct dimensions. The files are almost ready to move.

Almost. There is still the question of what exactly
the platform expects you to upload — and the
answer is more specific than most authors expect.

The Files Publishing Platforms Expect

Your manuscript is formatted. Your page count is confirmed. Your cover is built to the correct dimensions. Now you need to hand KDP the actual files.

This is simpler than it sounds. You are providing two things: the interior of the book and the cover. Everything else is just the format those two pieces take.

Print Interior — Use PDF

For your print interior, upload a PDF. Not a DOCX. Not an RTF. A PDF.

KDP accepts DOCX files for print interiors and will convert them automatically. The conversion usually works. It also sometimes introduces spacing changes, font substitutions, or page count shifts that you did not intend and may not notice until the previewer shows you something unexpected. A PDF locks your layout exactly as you built it. What you see in your formatted document is what KDP prints. No surprises.

Export your interior as PDF from whatever tool you used to format it. In Word or LibreOffice, go to File, then Export as PDF or Save as PDF. In Atticus, the export function handles this directly. In Kindle Create, the export step produces the correct file automatically.

Ebook Interior — EPUB or Let KDP Convert

For ebooks, the standard file format is EPUB. Most formatting tools export EPUB directly. If yours does, use it.

If you do not have an EPUB and you do not want to create one, KDP will convert your DOCX to ebook format automatically. For a straightforward nonfiction manuscript with standard formatting, the auto-conversion works reasonably well. For anything with complex layout, tables, or heavy image use, format the ebook intentionally rather than relying on conversion.

Check the ebook preview after upload regardless of how you created the file. The conversion process occasionally scrambles spacing or drops formatting that looked correct in the source document.

Cover Files

Your print cover is a full wraparound PDF — front, spine, and back in a single file, built to the exact dimensions KDP calculated for your page count and trim size. This file must be exported at 300 DPI. Lower resolution will either be rejected or will print poorly.

Your ebook cover is just the front cover image, uploaded as a JPG or PNG. No spine, no back cover. Keep the resolution high — KDP recommends at least 2560 pixels on the longest side.

The Atticus Advantage Here

If you formatted in Atticus, this step is where it earns its cost. Atticus exports both the print PDF and the ebook EPUB in one step, correctly formatted for each format. You do not have to manage separate workflows for print and ebook. You export once and you have both files ready to upload.

That is its strongest practical argument. Not the formatting itself — other tools format just as well — but the clean dual export.

Name Your Files Like You Have 25 Books

This sounds minor and is not minor at all.

Name every file with the title, the version, and the format before you upload anything. Something like CalmWay_Interior_v3_PRINT.pdf or CalmWay_Cover_FINAL.pdf. Not Document1. Not interior_final_FINAL_v2_USE THIS ONE.

You will have multiple versions of these files before you are done. You will come back to this book months later to make a correction and you will need to know which file is which without opening all of them. Name them clearly now. It takes ten seconds and saves real confusion later.

The Previewer Is the Last Check

Once the files are uploaded, KDP generates a preview. Use it. Flip through every page. Check that chapter titles landed correctly, no blank pages appeared that should not be there, images did not shift, and the cover wraps correctly front to back.

If something is wrong, fix the source file, export again, and re-upload. This is normal. Most authors go through at least two upload cycles before everything looks right. The previewer exists precisely for this. Trust it over everything else, including how the file looked on your screen before upload.

When the previewer looks right, you are ready for the next step.

Part IV

The Upload

Inside the KDP Dashboard

This is the moment that makes many authors hesitate.

Not because it is especially complicated, but because it feels official. Up to this point the book has lived on your computer. You have revised it, formatted it, designed the cover, and exported the files. The project has been real, but private.

Uploading the book changes that.

Now the manuscript is about to enter the world.

The good news is that the KDP upload process is more straightforward than it looks from the outside. The dashboard contains a lot of fields, but they are simply asking for information you already have. The key is understanding that the process happens in three sections, not all at once.

The Three Pages

Page 1 — Book Details

Page 2 — Content

Page 3 — Pricing

Each page focuses on a different part of the process. Thinking of the upload this way keeps the steps organized and prevents the feeling that everything is happening at once.

What You Can Fix Later vs. What You Really Don't Want to Get Wrong

Before you start filling in fields, here is the most useful thing to understand about the KDP dashboard: almost everything is editable after publication. Most authors do not know this. They treat every field like it is carved in stone and panic accordingly. It is not. You can go back.

That said, some fields are significantly more painful to change than others, and a couple of them have downstream consequences that are worth getting right the first time.

These fields are easy to change any time and take effect quickly. Keywords — you can update all seven slots from your KDP bookshelf whenever you want. Description — rewrite it as many times as you like. Price — change it today, it updates within hours. Categories — you can request changes by contacting KDP support. Author bio on your Author Central page — edit it directly any time.

These fields can be changed but require more care. The title and subtitle can be edited, but changes trigger a review process and temporarily affect your book's search history and ranking. Change them if they are wrong, but do not treat them as a first draft you will fix later. Get them right before you publish.

These are the fields you really do not want to get wrong. Your ISBN — once assigned to a specific title and format in Bowker and entered in KDP, changing it is complicated and sometimes impossible without unpublishing. Your imprint — must match Bowker exactly or KDP rejects the ISBN entirely. Your trim size — if you need to change the trim size after publishing, you have to upload a completely reformatted interior and a new cover built to the new dimensions. It is not impossible but it is a significant amount of rework. Your author name as it appears on the cover — this feeds into your Author Central profile and your catalog. Inconsistencies here fragment your author page and confuse readers looking for your other books.

Know which category each field falls into before you start. Move quickly through the easy ones. Slow down for the ones that matter.

Page 1 — Book Details

The first page asks for information about the book itself. None of the fields are technical. They simply describe the book.

You will enter things like title, subtitle, author name, book description, keywords, and categories.

If you worked through the earlier chapters of this book, most of these decisions are already made. This is where they get entered into the system.

One important note about the description: it is not a summary of the book. It is a short piece of persuasive writing designed to help a potential reader decide whether the book is worth their time. Think of it as the conversation happening on the back cover.

This page also asks for your ISBN and publisher imprint. Which brings us to something nobody warns you about.

The ISBN and Imprint Problem

If you purchased your own ISBN through Bowker — which you should, because owning your own ISBN means you control your publishing record — there is a step most publishing guides skip entirely: you have to register the ISBN in Bowker before you ever open KDP.

Bowker is the official ISBN agency for the United States. When you buy an ISBN, it starts as unassigned. Before it is useful to anyone, including KDP, you have to log into your Bowker account, find the ISBN, and fill out the registration fields. Until you do that, the ISBN is just a number. It is not attached to your book.

Here is what Bowker asks for when you register an ISBN, and what to put in each field.

Title and subtitle. Enter them exactly as they appear on your cover. Every word, every colon, every capitalization. This is not the place for a working title or an approximation.

Description. This field trips up a lot of authors because it sounds like a summary. It is not. Write it like a back cover blurb — lead with the reader's problem, tell them what the book delivers, close with a reason to read it. You get 350 words. Most strong descriptions use 100 to 150. A wall of plot summary is not a description. A pitch is a description.

Subjects and genres. Bowker gives you two genre slots. Be specific. For a nonfiction book about self-publishing, your first genre is Language Arts and Disciplines / Publishing. Your second might be Business and Economics / Small Business and Entrepreneurship. Do not pick General Nonfiction and call it done. The more specific your genre assignment, the more useful the ISBN record is to booksellers and libraries that rely on Bowker data.

Author bio. Keep it short. Two or three sentences: who you are, what you write, what gives you credibility on this topic. This is not your full author biography. It is the version that fits in a database field.

Target audience. Bowker asks who the book is for. Be specific here too. "General adult" is technically accurate for most nonfiction but tells nobody anything. Describe the actual reader: adults navigating self-publishing for the first time, or first-time authors who have finished a manuscript and don't know what comes next.

Format. You are registering this ISBN for a specific format — paperback, hardcover, or ebook.

A paperback and an ebook of the same title are two different ISBNs. Register them separately. Do not assign a paperback ISBN to an ebook or vice versa.

Once you submit, the status will show as Pending. That is normal. Bowker typically flips it to Assigned within 24 hours, sometimes faster. Do not try to use the ISBN in KDP while it is still Pending. KDP checks against Bowker's database, and if the record has not propagated yet, you will get a mismatch error that has nothing to do with anything you did wrong.

Wait for Assigned. Then wait another 24 to 48 hours for the record to fully propagate to KDP's systems. Yes, that means you may be waiting up to 48 hours after the Assigned status appears before KDP recognizes it. This is not a bug. It is just how the two systems sync.

Now, the part that actually causes problems in KDP.

When you registered your ISBN, Bowker asked for a publisher name. That publisher name is your imprint. Whatever you typed in that field — your LLC name, your publishing imprint, or your own personal name — is what KDP expects to see in the imprint field during upload. Exactly. Not approximately. Not close enough. Exactly.

KDP compares what you enter against what Bowker has on file. If there is any discrepancy — a missing comma, a different capitalization, LLC where Bowker has just your name, or your name where Bowker has your company — the system will reject it.

Here is the thing nobody mentions: many first-time authors registered their ISBN under their own name because that is what Bowker asked for first and they filled it in without thinking. Not their LLC. Not their imprint. Their name. So if your company is called Sunrise Harbor Press but you registered the ISBN under Jane Doe, KDP wants Jane Doe in that field. Not Sunrise Harbor Press.

Log into your Bowker account. Find the ISBN. Read the publisher name exactly as it appears. Copy that into KDP. Do not type it from memory. Copy it.

Page 2 — Content

This is the page where the actual book files get uploaded.

You will see fields for the manuscript file, the cover file, and print settings for paperbacks.

For a print book, KDP expects the manuscript as a PDF or DOCX file and the cover as a PDF file that includes the front, spine, and back as a single wraparound image.

After the files upload, KDP generates a previewer. The previewer shows how the book will appear when printed. You can flip through the pages, check the layout, and confirm that the cover lines up correctly.

Take a few minutes here. Do not skip the previewer.

What the Previewer Will Tell You

The previewer is where first-time authors meet errors they could not have seen on their own computer.

The most common one involves page size. You told KDP you want a 6-inch by 9-inch book. But your word processor may have been set to a different size all along — US Letter, which is 8.5 by 11 inches, is the default in most applications. The document looks perfectly normal on your screen. The margins look fine. The text looks fine. There is nothing visible that tells you anything is wrong.

KDP's previewer is the first thing that actually checks whether your file matches the trim size you selected. If it does not match, you will see an error. You will need to go back into the document, fix the page size, reformat, export a new file, and upload again.

This is not a failure. It is a discovery. The previewer exists precisely to catch these things before the book goes to print.

The Page Count Problem

Once your interior file is accepted, KDP calculates the exact number of pages in your book. Write that number down.

The page count determines the spine width of your cover. The spine width determines the total dimensions of the cover file. If your cover was built before you had a confirmed page count, there is a reasonable chance the dimensions will not match.

This is why the sequence matters. Finalize the interior completely — correct page size, correct margins, correct formatting, all front matter in place — before you build the cover. Every formatting change you make after that point can change the page count, which changes the spine, which means the cover needs to be rebuilt.

The formula KDP uses for spine width is simple: multiply the page count by 0.002252 inches for white paper. A 130-page book has a spine of roughly 0.29 inches. A 200-page book has a spine of roughly 0.45 inches. Small difference on paper. Significant difference when a cover built for 200 pages gets uploaded for a 130-page book.

If the previewer tells you that your expected cover size is 12.545 by 9.250 inches but your submitted file is 12.467 by 9.247 inches, that is the spine telling you it was built for a different page count. Fix the cover dimensions to match exactly what KDP specifies for your actual page count. Not approximately. Exactly.

The Cover Rebuild Loop

Most authors upload the cover more than once. Sometimes several times.

The first upload fails because the dimensions are off. You fix the dimensions and upload again. Then the previewer flags that your content is too close to the edge of the safe zone. You adjust and upload again. Then the spine text is too small to read. You fix it and upload again.

This is normal. It is not a sign that you are doing something wrong. It is the previewer doing its job, which is to catch problems before they become permanent.

The honest version of "most authors go through this process once or twice" is this: most authors go through it more than that, and the ones who go through it least are the ones who finalized their interior before they built their cover.

The Gutter Margin

One more thing the previewer may flag: the gutter.

The gutter is the inside margin — the edge of the page that runs along the spine. For a book that will be physically bound and opened by readers, the gutter needs to be wide enough that text does not disappear into the binding.

KDP specifies minimum gutter requirements based on page count. For books in the 100 to 200 page range, KDP typically requires a gutter of at least 0.375 inches. If your interior was formatted with a zero gutter or a very small one, the previewer will flag it. The fix is straightforward: go back into the document, increase the gutter margin, reformat, export, and upload again.

Page 3 — Pricing

The final page focuses on how the book will be sold. Here you will set the price, choose distribution options, and select the territories where the book will be available.

For most independent authors, the simplest approach is to make the book available worldwide. Unless you have a specific reason to restrict distribution to certain regions, broader availability costs nothing and opens more potential readers.

Pricing is flexible. You can change it after publication. Do not spend too long trying to find the perfect number. Look at comparable books in your category, pick a reasonable price, and move on. You can always adjust later.

Once pricing is set, the system performs a final review. And then the button appears. That part comes next.

Metadata Fields Explained

Back in Chapter 4 we talked about what metadata is and why Amazon weighs it the way it does. This chapter is different. This one is practical.

By the time you reach this point in the KDP dashboard, you are tired. You have been formatting files and rebuilding covers and double-checking margins. The last thing you want is to slow down and think carefully about a text field.

Do it anyway.

The metadata you enter here is what the algorithm uses to find your readers. A book with a strong interior and weak metadata is a book that exists in a warehouse nobody visits. Get this part right.

Title and Subtitle

These fields should already be locked. You worked through them in Chapter 3.

Enter them here exactly as they appear on your cover. Not approximately. Exactly. If your cover says "The Calm Way to Publish a Book" then that is what goes in the title field. Every word, every colon, every capitalization — it should match.

The same goes for subtitle. Word for word.

If there is any discrepancy between your cover and your KDP title fields, Amazon may flag it during review. More importantly, it confuses readers who see different versions of the title in different places. Consistency is not a style preference here. It is functional.

Author Name

Enter your name exactly as it appears on every other book in your catalog.

If this is your first book, decide now how you want your name to appear and use that format from this point forward. Changing it later is possible but creates friction — Amazon treats different name formats as different authors, which fragments your catalog in search results.

The Description Field

This is the one that matters most after the title.

Your description is not a summary. Summaries tell readers what the book contains. Descriptions convince readers who are already looking at the page to actually buy it. These are different goals and they require different writing.

Here is the distinction in practice.

A summary reads like: "This book covers the publishing process from manuscript to launch, including formatting, metadata, cover design, and the KDP dashboard."

A description reads like: "You finished the manuscript. Now what? This book walks you through exactly what comes next — in the order it actually needs to happen — so you can stop guessing and start publishing."

One of those tells a reader what the book is. The other tells them why they need it.

Write the description like the reader is standing in a bookstore, holding your book, deciding whether to put it back on the shelf. You have about thirty seconds. What do you say?

A few practical things about the description field:

It supports basic HTML formatting. Amazon's KDP description box accepts a small set of HTML tags — bold, italics, paragraph breaks, and a few others. Use paragraph breaks. A wall of text does not perform as well as text with visible structure. Bold your most important line, usually the one that most clearly states what the reader gets.

Lead with the reader's problem. Open with the situation your reader is already in. If your book is for first-time self-publishers, open with the feeling of finishing the manuscript and not knowing what comes next. You are reflecting their reality back at them before you introduce your solution.

Be specific. Vague descriptions do not convert. "A comprehensive guide to publishing" tells the reader nothing. "A step-by-step walkthrough of the KDP dashboard, from cover upload to pricing" tells them something specific they can evaluate.

End with momentum. The last line of the description should give the reader a reason to click Buy. Not a hard sell. Just a clear statement of what happens when they read this book.

The description can be up to 4,000 characters. Most effective descriptions run between 150 and 300 words. Longer is not better. Clearer is better.

Keywords

You get seven keyword fields. Each one can hold a short phrase — up to 50 characters.

Do not repeat words that are already in your title or subtitle. Amazon already indexes those. Putting the same words in your keyword fields wastes slots you could use to reach readers who search differently.

Fill all seven. Leaving fields empty is leaving discoverability on the table.

Think in phrases the way a reader would type them. Not "publishing" but "how to self-publish a book." Not "KDP" but "KDP publishing guide for beginners." The longer and more specific the phrase, the more likely it matches what an actual reader types into the search bar when they are looking for exactly what you wrote.

You can change keywords at any time from your KDP bookshelf. This is not a permanent decision. If something is not working after 30 to 60 days, adjust and see what changes.

Categories

You chose two categories. Enter them here.

If you are not sure which categories to select, go back to Chapter 4. The short version: pick categories that are specific enough to give you a realistic chance of showing up, and accurate enough that readers who find you actually want your book.

A book that ranks well in the wrong category does not sell. A book that ranks modestly in the right category does.

Once all of these fields are complete, you move to the content upload page. That is where the files go in and the previewer tells you what actually happened.

Everything you enter on this page works quietly in the background from the day the book goes live. The care you put into it now is not just a setup task. It is an investment in every day the book exists in the store.

Pricing, Territories, and Royalties

At some point during the KDP setup process, you will arrive at the pricing page and realize that nobody ever explained how any of this actually works.

The royalty structure, the territory options, the price fields — it all appears at once, right when you are tired and just want to be done.

This chapter explains it plainly so you can make a decision and move on.

How Royalties Work

KDP offers two royalty rates for ebooks: 35% and 70%.

The 70% rate sounds obviously better. It usually is. But it comes with conditions.

To qualify for the 70% royalty, the ebook must be priced between $2.99 and $9.99. It must also be enrolled in KDP Select, or priced at least 20% below the lowest price you have set on any other platform.

If your ebook is priced below $2.99 or above $9.99, Amazon pays 35% regardless of anything else.

For print books, the royalty structure is different. KDP pays 60% of the list price, minus the printing cost. The printing cost depends on page count, paper type, and whether the book is in color. A standard black and white paperback in the 150 to 300 page range typically costs between three and six dollars to print. Whatever is left after that cost is subtracted from your 60% is your royalty.

This is why pricing a print book too low can result in very small royalties or even no royalty at all. KDP will not let you set a price below the minimum required to cover printing costs, but it is worth understanding the math so you are not surprised by what shows up in your dashboard.

The Actual Math

Here is a simple example for a print book.

Your book is 200 pages, black and white, 6 by 9 inches. KDP estimates the printing cost at roughly $3.85. You set the price at $14.99.

Your royalty is 60% of $14.99, which is $8.99, minus the $3.85 printing cost. That leaves $5.14 per copy sold on Amazon.

If you set the price at $9.99, the math changes. 60% of $9.99 is $5.99, minus $3.85 printing cost, leaving $2.14 per copy.

Neither number is wrong. It depends on what you are trying to do. A lower price may sell more copies. A higher price may earn more per copy. There is no universal right answer, and you can change the price after publication if the first number does not feel right.

Here is the trap nobody warns you about. KDP will not let you set a price below the minimum required to cover printing costs. But it will let you set a price just barely above that minimum, which can result in a royalty of almost nothing. If you price a 300-page book at $8.99 and the printing cost is $6.40, your 60% is $5.39, minus $6.40 printing cost — which means you owe more than you earn. KDP will flag this and enforce a minimum, but authors who price without doing the math first are often surprised to discover their royalty is $0.18 or $0.43 per copy. Use the royalty calculator on the KDP pricing page before you finalize any number. It does the math for you in real time.

Territories

KDP asks which territories you want to make the book available in. The options are essentially: worldwide, or specific countries.

Unless you have a specific reason to restrict the book — a pre-existing deal with a publisher in certain regions, a legal issue, something unusual — select worldwide.

Restricting territories costs you nothing to avoid and potentially costs you sales if you get it wrong.

Broader is better unless you have a reason for otherwise. Most independent authors publishing their first book have no reason to restrict. Select worldwide and move on.

Pricing Strategy Without the Overthinking

New authors tend to underprice out of insecurity and overprice out of optimism. Neither extreme serves them well.

The practical approach is simple: look at what comparable books in your category are selling for. Not the outliers at the top or bottom, but the middle of the range. Price your book there.

For nonfiction paperbacks in the practical or self-help space, $12.99 to $16.99 is a typical range. For shorter books under 150 pages, $9.99 to $12.99 is common. For longer, more comprehensive titles, $17.99 to $24.99 is not unusual.

For ebooks, $2.99 to $7.99 covers most independent nonfiction. Staying in that range keeps you in the 70% royalty bracket and keeps the price accessible enough that it does not become a barrier.

Pick a number in the reasonable range. You are not signing a contract. If it turns out to be wrong, you fix it.

KDP Select

At some point during setup, KDP will offer you the option to enroll in KDP Select.

KDP Select gives your ebook access to Kindle Unlimited, where subscribers can read it as part of their subscription and you earn per page read. It also gives you access to promotional tools like free book days and Kindle Countdown Deals.

The catch is exclusivity. Enrolling in KDP Select means you cannot sell or distribute the ebook version anywhere else — no other retailers, no your own website, nowhere. The enrollment period is 90 days and renews automatically unless you opt out.

For authors who want to be on multiple platforms — Apple Books, Barnes and Noble, Kobo, Google Play — KDP Select is not compatible with that goal.

For authors who want to be Amazon-only, at least to start, KDP Select is worth considering.

Neither choice is permanent. You can enroll, try it for 90 days, and opt out if it is not working. You can also skip it entirely and distribute wide from the beginning. It is a business decision, not a moral one. Make it based on where your readers are and how you want to distribute. Then move on.

Part V

The Moment of Publication

Hitting Publish

At some point during the upload process, after the file rejections and the cover rebuilds and the margin corrections and the ISBN mismatches, a thought will occur to you.

Maybe the vanity publisher wasn't so bad.

Maybe paying someone else to handle all of this was actually reasonable. Maybe the $5,000 or $10,000 or $20,000 was not a scam so much as a fee for not having to know what a gutter margin is.

This thought is normal. It visits almost everyone who publishes independently for the first time.

Here is what is also true: the vanity publisher would have taken your money, formatted the book incorrectly, uploaded it with the wrong metadata, kept most of the royalties, and handed you a contract that made it nearly impossible to leave.

You are not paying for someone to handle it. You are learning to handle it yourself. That is a different thing entirely.

Push through the thought. The button is close.

What You Have Done to Get Here

By the time you reach the publish button, you have made dozens of decisions that most authors never fully understand.

You chose a trim size and formatted the interior to match it. You caught the page size error that your word processor hid from you for the entire drafting process. You calculated spine width. You rebuilt the cover when the dimensions changed. You fixed the gutter. You matched your imprint to your Bowker record exactly. You waited the 48 hours.

None of that is small. Most authors who go through a vanity publisher never learn any of it, which means they cannot fix it when something goes wrong, and they cannot do it better the next time.

You can.

One Final Check Before You Click

Before you press the button, do a fast pass on the fields that matter most.

Title and subtitle — match exactly what is on the cover and exactly what is in Bowker. Author name — consistent with every other book in your catalog. ISBN and imprint — log into Bowker one more time, read the publisher name, confirm it matches KDP character for character. You already did this. Check it anyway. Categories and keywords — specific, deliberate, no repeats from the title.

You covered all of these in detail earlier. This is not a second lesson. It is a pre-flight check. Thirty seconds. Then move on.

The Previewer, One More Time

If you have not already done a thorough pass through the KDP previewer, do it now.

Flip to the first page. Check that it is a right-hand page. Flip to the table of contents. Check that the page numbers populated correctly. Flip to the first chapter. Check that the heading style looks right and the body text is readable. Flip to the last page. Make sure nothing got cut off.

Check the cover. Front, spine, back. Make sure the spine text is legible and centered. Make sure the back cover content is inside the safe zone and nothing is getting clipped at the edges.

If something is wrong, fix it now. Uploading a corrected file after publication is possible but it adds time and means the book is briefly unavailable during the update.

If everything looks right, you are ready.

The Button

The publish button does not feel as dramatic as you might expect.

After everything it took to get here — the writing, the revision, the formatting, the cover design, the upload process, the error messages, the corrections, the waiting — the final act is a single click on a button that says Publish Your Paperback Book.

Or Publish Your Kindle eBook.

Or both, if you are doing them at the same time.

Click it.

The system will confirm that your book has been submitted for review. You will get a confirmation email. The review process will begin. And then, for a few hours or a couple of days, you wait.

What Happens While You Wait

Amazon's review process typically takes 24 to 72 hours. Sometimes faster. Occasionally longer if there is a flag that requires human review.

During this time the book will show up in your KDP bookshelf with a status of In Review. This is normal. Do not resubmit. Do not make changes to the listing. Do not upload a new file because you noticed a typo on page 47. Just wait.

Here is what most authors actually do while waiting: they refresh the KDP dashboard every twenty minutes, they read their own manuscript looking for things they wish they had changed, they check Amazon to see if the book is live yet, and they start second-guessing the title, the cover, the description, and approximately every decision they made in the last three months.

This is normal and it is not useful. The book is in review. You cannot change anything meaningful right now. What you can do is write the next one, tell a few people the book is coming, set up or update your Author Central page, and get some sleep.

If the review finds an issue, Amazon will send you an email explaining what needs to be corrected. Read it carefully. The errors are usually specific and fixable. Make the correction, upload the revised file, and resubmit. This is not a rejection of your book. It is a technical flag. Fix the thing it specifies and move on.

If the review passes, the book goes live. You will get another email. The product page will appear in the Amazon store. The sales rank will be an enormous number because it starts at the bottom and climbs with sales. The reviews section will be empty.

At that point, you have published a book.

The Feeling After

Some authors feel elated. Some feel strangely flat. Most feel both at the same time.

The elation makes sense. You finished something real. A book exists in the world that did not exist before. Anyone with an internet connection and a few dollars can find it, buy it, and read it. That is not nothing.

The flatness also makes sense. You have been building toward this moment for months. Now it has arrived, and the world has not stopped to acknowledge it. The Amazon page looks like every other Amazon page. The sales rank is an enormous number. The reviews section is empty.

This is the gap between finishing and succeeding, and it is where most authors lose momentum.

The book being published is not the end of the process. It is the beginning of a different one. That is what the next chapter is about.

What Actually Matters After Launch

The book is live. The hard part is over.

Except now a different kind of hard part begins.

Publication is not the finish line. It is the starting line for a different race. The writing got the book into existence. Everything that happens next determines whether anyone finds it.

This chapter is about what actually moves the needle — and what does not, no matter how much time authors spend on it.

The Things Authors Panic About That Do Not Matter

A few things will happen after publication that may cause unnecessary stress. Here is a short list of things that are not worth losing sleep over.

The sales rank will look alarming at first. Every new book starts with no rank or a very high number, which means very few sales. This is expected. A brand new book with no reviews and no promotion is not going to immediately appear on bestseller lists. That is not failure. That is physics.

The cover may look slightly different on the product page than it did in the previewer. Screen color rendering varies. If it looked good in the previewer, it will look good in print. Trust the process.

You will find a typo. Probably within the first hour of the book going live. This is a universal law of publishing. You can fix it — KDP allows you to upload a corrected file at any time — but it is worth knowing that readers are remarkably tolerant of the occasional imperfection. The book will not be ruined by one misplaced comma.

Someone may leave a review you did not expect. Reviews are outside your control. The goal is to write the best book you can and let readers respond honestly. That is the deal.

What Does Not Move the Needle

Start here, because this list is longer than most authors expect.

Refreshing your sales dashboard does not move the needle. Checking your rank every hour does not change it. Watching the numbers is not the same as influencing them. Check your dashboard once a day at most, and only if you can look at it without spiraling.

Posting about your book on social media once and hoping it spreads does not move the needle. A single post reaches people who already know you. Most of them will like it and not buy it. That is not a failure of your book. That is how social media works.

Worrying about your cover after publication does not move the needle. If the cover was good enough to get through the previewer and into the store, it is good enough. You can update it later if you have real evidence that it is the problem. Anxiety is not evidence.

Getting one bad review does not move the needle. One bad review on an otherwise quiet book is meaningless. Readers who are genuinely interested in your topic will read the book and form their own opinion. Do not respond to negative reviews. Do not obsess over them. Move on.

Changing the price every week does not move the needle. Pricing affects conversion, but constant changes signal instability and make it harder to run promotions effectively. Set a price, give it at least 30 days, then evaluate.

What Actually Moves the Needle

Discoverability is the engine. Everything else is noise.

Your categories and keywords are working in the background every day, connecting your book to readers who are actively searching for what you wrote. If you chose them carefully before publication, they are already doing their job. If you chose them quickly just to get through the setup screen, go back and update them. KDP allows you to change categories and keywords at any time from your bookshelf.

Your book description is your silent salesperson. It is on your product page every hour of every day, either converting browsers into buyers or failing to. Read it again now that the book is live. Does it make someone want to read the book? Does it tell them clearly who the book is for and what they will get from it? If the answer is no, rewrite it. This is one of the highest-leverage things you can do after launch.

Reviews matter, but not in the way most authors think. A book with ten honest reviews converts better than a book with zero reviews. The reviews do not need to be five stars. They need to exist. Ask people who have read the book to leave an honest review. Not a favor. An honest one. Readers trust honest reviews. They can spot the ones that are not.

Ads can work, but only after the basics are right. If your cover is weak, your description is unclear, or your categories are wrong, running ads will accelerate the failure, not fix it. Get the product page right first. Then consider ads.

The Long Game

The single most effective marketing tool for an independent author is a second book.

And a third.

Readers who find one book and like it look for more. A catalog of books creates a flywheel effect that a single title cannot. Each new book brings new readers, and some percentage of those readers will go back and buy the earlier ones.

This does not mean rushing. A bad book released quickly does more damage than a good book released slowly. But it does mean that the time you spend obsessing over the launch of book one would almost always be better spent writing book two.

The authors who build sustainable independent publishing careers are almost never the ones who had a single breakout launch. They are the ones who kept writing, kept publishing, and let the catalog do the work over time.

The Practical Post-Launch Checklist

Once the book is live, here is what is actually worth your time.

Verify the product page. Make sure the cover looks right, the description is formatted correctly, the categories are showing up as expected, and the look inside preview is displaying cleanly.

Share it once, genuinely. Tell your actual audience — your email list, your readers, the people who have been waiting for this — that the book is available. Not a campaign. Just a real announcement.

Ask for reviews. Identify five to ten people who you know have read or will read the book and ask them directly to leave an honest review. Make it easy by sending them the link.

Update your author page. Amazon gives every KDP author an Author Central page. If you have not set it up, do it now. Add a photo, a bio, and links to all your books. Readers who want to know more about you will land there.

Then start writing the next one.

What This Book Was

This book was a sequence.

Not a guarantee. Not a formula. A sequence.

Manuscript. Revision. Title. Cover. Format. Metadata. Upload. Publish.

Done in that order, with attention at each step, independent publishing is manageable. The technology is not the obstacle. The confusion about what comes next is the obstacle. And now you know what comes next.

The next book will be easier. The one after that easier still. The process that felt overwhelming the first time becomes routine. The errors you made become chapters in the book you write for the next person who needs a map.

You have the map now.

Use it.

The Calm Publishing Checklist

Use this checklist each time you publish a book. Nothing here is optional. Nothing here is in the wrong order.

The Manuscript

1. Draft is complete

2. Revision pass complete — content, structure, flow

3. Proofread — grammar, spelling, punctuation

4. Front matter in place: title page, copyright page, also by page, table of contents

5. Back matter in place: appendices, resources, author bio

The Title and Metadata

6. Title locked and final

7. Subtitle locked and final

8. Title and subtitle consistent across: cover, KDP dashboard, Bowker

9. Book description written — persuasive, not a summary

10. Two categories selected — specific, accurate

11. Seven keyword fields filled — no repeats from title or subtitle

12. Author name consistent with all other titles in your catalog

The ISBN — Bowker Registration

13. ISBN purchased through Bowker — paperback and ebook are separate ISBNs, buy both

14. Bowker registration form completed for each ISBN — not just purchased, actually filled out

15. Title and subtitle entered in Bowker exactly as they appear on the cover

16. Bowker description written as a pitch, not a summary — lead with the reader's problem

17. Subjects and genres assigned — specific subcategories, not General Nonfiction

18. Author bio entered — two to three sentences, who you are and what you write

19. Target audience specified — describe the actual reader, not just "general adult"

20. Format confirmed — paperback ISBN assigned to paperback only, ebook ISBN to ebook only

21. Status shows Assigned in Bowker — do not proceed while still Pending

22. Waited additional 24 to 48 hours after Assigned for KDP systems to sync

The ISBN — KDP Entry

23. Publisher name copied directly from Bowker — do not type from memory

24. Imprint in KDP matches Bowker publisher name character for character

25. If KDP rejects the ISBN — check Bowker first, confirm Assigned, wait, then try again

The Cover

26. Interior page count confirmed from KDP previewer

27. Spine width calculated using confirmed page count

28. Cover dimensions match KDP specifications for your page count

29. Front cover: title, subtitle, author name all correct

30. Spine: title and author name legible at actual print size

31. Back cover: description compelling, barcode area clear

32. All text inside safe zone — nothing within 0.125 inches of edge

33. Cover exported as PDF at 300 DPI

The Interior File

34. Page size set to your trim size — not US Letter, not A4

35. Gutter margin set correctly for your page count

36. Outside, top, and bottom margins at least 0.75 inches

37. Font consistent throughout — no stray size or face changes

38. Chapter headings consistent style

39. Page numbers present and correct

40. Table of contents updated with correct page numbers

41. Blank page before each new part or section if required

42. Interior exported as PDF or saved as DOCX for upload

The Upload

43. Interior file uploaded to KDP

44. Cover file uploaded to KDP

45. KDP previewer reviewed — all pages checked

46. Cover preview checked — front, spine, back all correct

47. Page count confirmed from previewer — matches cover build

48. All metadata fields on Page 1 complete

49. Pricing set

50. Territories selected — worldwide unless you have a reason otherwise

51. KDP Select decision made

Publication

52. Final review of all fields before clicking publish

53. Publish button clicked

54. Confirmation email received

55. Book live in Amazon store — product page verified

56. Author Central page updated with new title

Post-Launch

57. Book description reviewed on live product page

58. Categories confirmed as showing correctly

59. Five to ten people asked for honest reviews

60. One genuine announcement made to your audience

The best thing you can do for this book is write the next one.